The Perceptive Peonies

written by **Sandra Rippetoe**   illustrated by **Joan Zehnder**

Nature's Rhyme
Harrodsburg, KY

The story text type was set in Gabriela

Library of Congress Control Number: 2021953491

ISBN: 979-8-9854114-2-3 (paperback)

ISBN: 979-8-9854114-3-0 (ebook)

Printed in the United States of America

About this Book

In the spring of 2021, I was happily working with a talented artist, Joan Zehnder, on a children's picture book titled *Dandelion Princess*. During a meeting, Joan told me about a set of twenty watercolor flower themed paintings which she had painted in years past. She wondered if I could write a story based on those paintings. I gratefully accepted the challenge! When I first saw the art, I was amazed that some of the flowers had detailed intricate human faces with such genuine emotional expressions. I studied the paintings, arranged them, stared at them, re-ordered them several times, and gazed some more. I thought about the peony characters before I went to sleep and when I woke up.

Once I began the actual writing, a story about grief and healing began to take shape. I guess I shouldn't be surprised by the emergence of this topic since at the time a covid-19 pandemic had raged around the entire globe for more than a year. Each day the news headlines announced more illness, suffering, and lives lost.

My sincere wish is that this story can provide a moment of hope, comfort, and perhaps insight during this overwhelmingly sad time in our beloved world.

I am so grateful to Joan for the opportunity to develop a story in this unique way. I'm appreciative of her generosity and creativity. I love the way she merges the natural world and human world in her paintings which, to me, depicts the interdependent web of life. Her artistic expressions speak to my heart, mind, and soul. Thanks so very much, Joan.

Sandra Rippetoe
December 27, 2021

A long time ago in a cottage made of stone,
a woman lived by herself but was never alone.
Here is her picture. Her name was Leone.

Leone spent her days in a magical place
with hundreds of peonies in a small garden space.

Look very carefully to see each flower's face
and listen as they talk . . . quiet voices with grace.

One summer day
Leone refused to come down.
The peonies heard sobbing —
such sadness profound.

Leone's tears flowed for weeks.
Time became a blur.
The peonies wondered,

"When will things be like they were?"

Sensitive Penelope covered her little ears —
to hear all that crying nearly moved her to tears.

Inquisitive Priscilla asked,
    "What can we do?
        To help her quit crying . . . .
            and remember joy she once knew?"

A conversation started
about sadness and grief.
One peony inquired,
"Does it relate to belief?"

"That life can get better?

That there's healing and hope?

That heartache can mend?

That indeed one can cope?"

"Remember how she'd curl up
for an afternoon nap?"
Pauline interrupted
who missed resting in Leone's lap.

Fun loving Pat joked,
"Leone hasn't laughed in a while.
I'll jump and surprise her!
That'll make her smile!"

Grandmother Tree spoke wisely, "I've seen this before.
Leone has to come out ... come out through a door. "

After thinking a minute, the tree shared a plan,
"You go first, dragonfly. Land on Leone's hand."

"Next, you two red birds, go perch on her window. Sing sweetly and loudly with one huge crescendo."

"Will this work?" Polly asked.
"I sure hope she'll look out.
'Cause she'll remember good times
when she sees us . . . no doubt!"

They acted on their plan the next day at sunrise.
It was a beautiful morn with bright painted skies.

They got Leone's attention. Toward the window she walked.
Kindhearted Pam waved, "Come out here and talk!"

"We miss you so much! You'll be happy again
if you come to the garden to be with your friends."

Leone went to the garden, responding to their call.
She glanced at the sky, but stared most of all . . .

at her dear peony flowers.
How they danced and performed!
How could she have forgotten?
They made her life charmed.

She felt moments of peace
as she looked at each one.
Yet her tears lingered,
her grief not yet done.

But when enough time passed, Leone's grief fully healed
and the magic of a garden was powerfully revealed.

Flowers still bloom in the midst of deep strife
and perceptive peonies understand a lot about life.

Sandra Rippetoe, MA, RDN, LD is a poet, author, registered dietitian nutritionist, and former homeschool teacher. Sandra loves spending time outdoors in nature. She's especially fond of the birds, bees, and butterflies found in yards. She's the author of another children's book, *Dandelion Princess*. Sandra lives in Kentucky with her husband and son. Please visit her online at naturesrhyme.com.

Joan Zehnder, MFA is an artist, author, teacher, and retired art therapist. Even as a child, Joan saw herself as an artist and spent many hours creating with crayons, watercolors, and pencils. She is the author of three books of paintings: *Imaginings*, *Threshold*, and *Creative Energy*, and the illustrator of another children's book, *Dandelion Princess*. For more information on Joan's art, please visit saatchiart.com/joanzehnder.

Made in United States
Orlando, FL
09 March 2022

15617522R00015